FOSSIL FUELS

POLLY GOODMAN

HODDER
Wayland

an imprint of Hodder Children's Books

LOOKING AT ENERGY

OTHER TITLES IN THE SERIES

Geothermal and Bio-energy · Nuclear Power
Solar Power · Water Power · Wind Power

This book is a simplified version of the title 'Fossil Fuels' in Hodder Wayland's 'Energy Forever?' series.

Language level consultant: Norah Granger
Editor: Belinda Hollyer   Designer: Jane Hawkins

Text copyright © 2001 Hodder Wayland
Volume copyright © 2001 Hodder Wayland

First published in 2001 by Hodder Wayland,
an imprint of Hodder Children's Books.

British Library Cataloguing in Publication Data
Goodman, Polly
Fossil fuels - (Looking at energy)
1.Fossil fuels - Juvenile literature
I.Title
333.8'2
ISBN 0 7502 3617 5

Printed and bound by G Canale & C.S.p.A.

Hodder Children's Books
A division of Hodder Headline Ltd
338 Euston Road, London NW1 3BH

Picture Acknowledgements
Cover: main picture Hodder Wayland Picture Library, miner Tony Stone/Mike Abrahams. US Department of Energy: pages 4 top, 16, 20, 43. Ecoscene: pages 15 (Gryniewicz), 24 (Erik Schaffer), 30, 30-31 (Sally Morgan), 32 (Gryniewicz), 36-37 (Alan Towse), 38 (Sally Morgan). Hodder Wayland Photo Library: pages 1 (BP), 18 (BP). Canada House: pages 6, 20-21. Mary Evans Photo Library: pages 8, 11, 12. Samfoto: pages 9 (Ragnar Frislid), 16 (Svein Erik Dahl), 20 right (Svein Erik Dahl), 23 (Hans Hvide Bang). Eye Ubiquitous: pages 13 (Steve Lindridge), 16-17 (David Cumming), 25 (Tim Hawkins), 28 (Davy Bold), 33 (J.B. Pickering), 37 (Paul Seheult). e.t. archive: page 10. Forlaget Flachs: pages 26-27 (Enequist Kommunikation), 35 (Olĕ Steen Hansen), 41 bottom and 43 bottom (Olĕ Steen Hansen), 41 top (D.O.N.G.). Shell Photo Service: page 29. Nissan Motors: page 34. National Coal Board: page 42. Science Photo Library: pages 4 bottom (Crown Copyright/ Health and Safety Laboratory), 5 (Simon Fraser), 43 top (Astrid & Hanns-Frieder Michler), 44 (Martin Bond), 45 (Martin Bond).

CONTENTS

WHAT ARE FOSSIL FUELS?

Fossil fuels are coal, oil and natural gas. We use these fuels for energy, for heating and lighting, and to drive machines. They are burned to release their energy.

Every day we use energy from fossil fuels. We burn coal, oil and gas in our homes for heating and cooking. Most of the electricity we use is made by power stations burning coal or oil.

Cars, buses and other vehicles burn petrol or diesel oil in their engines. We use them to travel from place to place.

▲ An oil-drilling tower at the Elk Hills oil field, in Alaska.

◄ A machine cuts coal inside an underground coal mine. The man in the front of the photo is measuring the noise level, to make sure it is not unsafe for the other workers.

Steam pours from the cooling towers of the Ferrybridge power station in Yorkshire, in Britain.

How were they formed?

Coal, oil and natural gas were formed over millions of years. They are made from the remains of plants and animals. Most coal began to form about 300 million years ago, when swamps covered much of the Earth. Tall plants grew in the swamps. When they died, they piled up together in layers. The layers became compressed (or squashed) one on top of the other.

As the layers became compressed, at first they formed peat. Then they formed lignite, or brown coal. Finally they formed anthracite, or black coal.

Oil and gas formed under the seas, from the remains of microscopic plants and animals. Under the sea, the compressed layers formed liquid oil, instead of coal. They also gave off gas. The oil and gas was trapped in pockets between the rocks around them. Now these areas are oil and gas fields.

FACTFILE

The youngest coal is lignite. When lignite is compressed, it gradually changes into different types of coal. Finally it changes into anthracite.

Anthracite coal can be up to 400 million years old. Lignite can be under 1 million years old.

◄ A machine digs up tar sands in Alberta, in Canada. Tar sands contain oil and gas, which can be extracted (or taken out) by mixing the sands with steam and water.

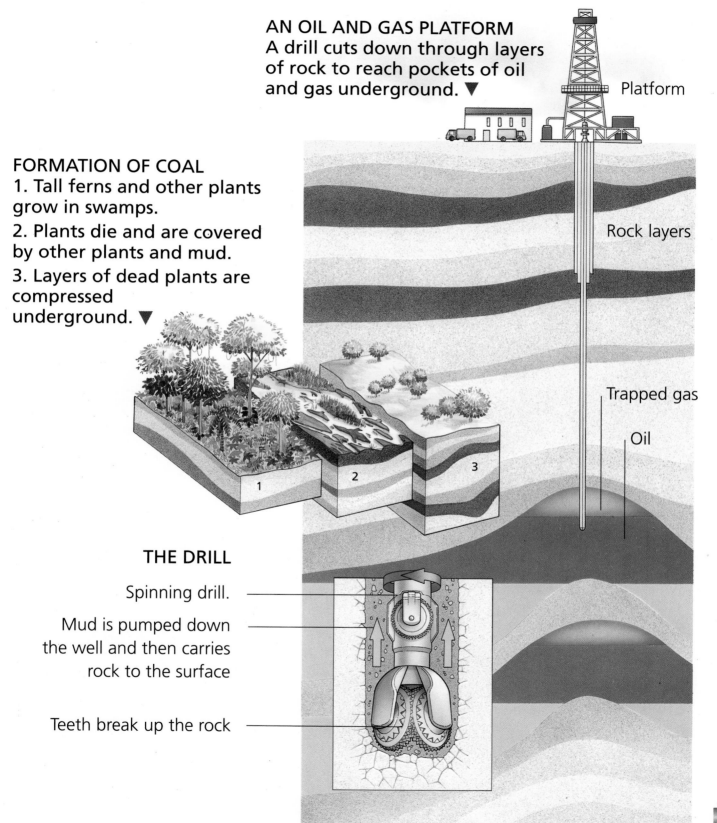

AN OIL AND GAS PLATFORM
A drill cuts down through layers of rock to reach pockets of oil and gas underground. ▼

Platform

FORMATION OF COAL
1. Tall ferns and other plants grow in swamps.
2. Plants die and are covered by other plants and mud.
3. Layers of dead plants are compressed underground. ▼

Rock layers

Trapped gas

Oil

1

2

3

THE DRILL

Spinning drill.

Mud is pumped down the well and then carries rock to the surface

Teeth break up the rock

FOSSIL FUELS IN HISTORY

Coal

Coal has been used for thousands of years. The first people to use it were probably the Chinese, about 3,000 years ago. Later, it was used by other ancient civilizations, including the Greeks and Romans in Europe, and the Hopi Indians in North America.

A drawing of a coal mine in 1885. There were no machines, so the miners used hand picks, shovels and horse-drawn carts to collect the coal. ▼

Steam engines were invented in the 1700s. They burned huge amounts of coal to make steam power. Steam engines ran machines in factories, so they helped the growth of industries in the 1800s. ▶

Mining

At first, coal was dug from hillsides and open pits using hand tools. By 300 AD, the Chinese were mining coal near the surface of the ground. In Europe, coal-mining started in the 1200s, but it was not until the 1600s that the industry really took off in Britain.

Until the 1600s, all coal-mining was done by hand. In the 1600s, ponies were taken down coal mines and used to pull carts full of coal. They were known as pit ponies. In the 1800s, steam engines were used to pump out water and pull up coal from the mines.

Oil

Like coal, oil has been used for thousands of years. The ancient Egyptians covered the bodies of their dead, called mummies, in thick oil hardened by the sunlight. Other ancient civilizations, such as the Chinese and the Native Americans, used oil for heat, light and medicine.

The Chinese first drilled oil in the second century BC. They used bamboo pipes and bronze tubes. But until the nineteenth century most oil was found in pools on the surface, or discovered by accident when digging wells.

The modern oil industry began in 1859 in the USA. Steam was used to power the drills.

The ribs and legs of an ancient Egyptian mummy, which has been covered in oil. ▶

In 1859, Edwin L. Drake first used steam power to drill for oil in Pennsylvania, in the USA. A few years later, drilling towers covered the hills of Pennsylvania.

▲ A lamplighter lights a gas street lamp in London, in 1867.

Gas

The ancient Chinese were the first people to use natural gas. They found it when they dug wells to look for salt water. They burned the gas to boil away the water and leave the salt behind.

In 1739, an English clergyman called John Clayton found out how to make gas from coal. In 1792, an English inventor first lit his home using coal gas. Soon after, many streets in Britain had lamps. The light was made from coal gas.

● Coal
● Oil
● Natural gas

This map shows the places where coal, oil and natural gas are found around the world. The most recent discoveries are gas fields in the North Sea, Russia, Canada, Australia and Algeria. ▶

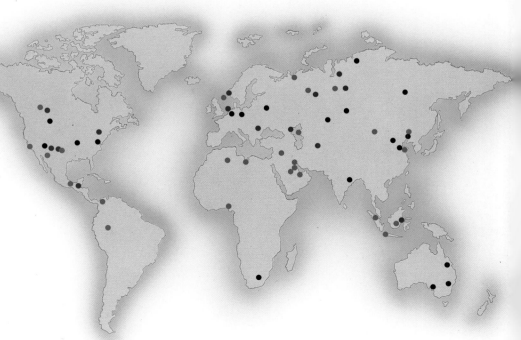

▲ A modern gas platform. The flame lets out bursts of gas.

Natural gas

The natural gas industry first started in the USA, in the middle of the nineteenth century. There were no long-distance pipelines to carry the gas very far, so people had to live close to the gas fields.

After 1930 steel pipelines were made, which could carry gas over long distances.

EXTRACTING FOSSIL FUELS

Before any drilling or mining begins, experts have to find stores of fossil fuels underground. In the past, this search relied on a lot of luck. Many wells were dug without success.

Today, scientists make a map of what is under the ground. This is called surveying. They look for certain types of rock that are likely to contain fossil fuels.

Some clues, such as the magnetic field and gravity of an area, give details about the type and density of rock underground. Explosions are used to measure how sound waves travel through rock. Samples of rock are drilled and studied.

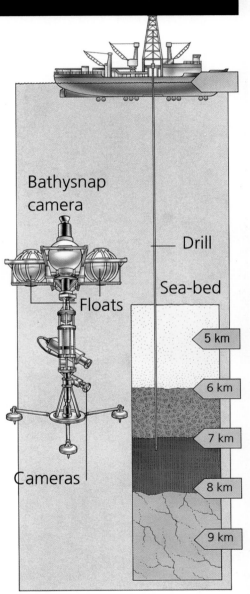

Bathysnap camera

Drill

Sea-bed

Floats

5 km

6 km

7 km

8 km

9 km

Cameras

▲ This diagram shows a ship doing a test drill for oil. The Bathysnap camera is dropped on to the sea-bed. After it has taken pictures, it floats to the surface.

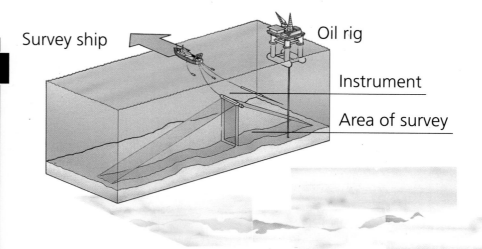

Survey ship · Oil rig · Instrument · Area of survey

▲ Survey ships take pictures of the sea-bed. They use a special instrument, which is dragged behind the ship.

Layers of sandstone and mudstone in Wales. These rocks are sedimentary rocks, like coal, but they formed earlier than coal.

Miners wear protective helmets with electric lamps. ▼

This huge drill is used to extract coal. As the drill turns, the teeth around its edge bite into the coal. ▼

Coal-mining

Modern coal-mining is done by machines, but people are still needed to operate them. The machines cut the coal, hold up the roof and carry coal and miners up and down the mine shaft.

If the coal is near the surface, it is mined from open pits. These are called open-cast mines. If the coal is over 60 metres below the ground, mines are dug deep underground.

At an open-cast mine in Germany coal is crushed, washed, and poured into piles.

When mines are dug underground, first a shaft is dug down to reach the coal. Miners dig outwards from the shaft.

After the coal has been cut, it is brought to the surface. Then it is blasted with explosives to separate it from the rock and crushed. Finally it is scooped up by huge shovels and washed.

FACTFILE

There are two main methods of underground mining. In longwall mining, the roof falls in behind the cutting machine. In room-and-pillar mining, the cutting machine leaves pillars of coal to hold up the roof.

Gas is carried to this terminal in Yorkshire, England, in pipelines from the North Sea.

Drilling for oil and gas

To reach oil and gas underground, a sharp, spinning drill cuts through the earth (see page 7). The drill is joined to a pipe. As the drill sinks under the ground, more pipe is added to the top. The pipe can be several kilometres long by the time the drill reaches oil or gas.

To help the drill cut through rock, liquid mud is pumped down the pipe. The mud washes away pieces of rock and helps drive the drill.

When the drill finally reaches the oil, it can let out a huge amount of pressure. The oil can burst out of the top of the pipe in a 'blow-out' or 'gusher'. Special valves at the top of the pipe stop blow-outs.

Water and gas can help force oil out of a well. A 'nodding donkey' machine forces steam into an oil well. The steam helps to push the oil up and out of the shaft. ▶

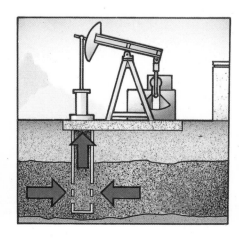

Offshore oil rigs

Oil under the sea-bed is drilled by offshore oil rigs. They can be as big as skyscrapers. In shallow seas, rigs stand on the sea-bed as far down as 400 metres below the surface of the water.

In deep water, rigs float on the surface, anchored to the sea-bed up to 1,000 metres below.

Drill ships can take oil from the deepest waters, as deep as 2,400 metres. They stay in exactly the same place using satellite navigation and special propellers. ▼

An offshore oil rig near the coast of Norway. Workers live at the top. ▶

This island was made
specially for an oil rig.
It is in the shallow
Beaufort Sea, near the
coast of Canada.

FACTFILE

The world's main
offshore oil fields are
under the Arabian Gulf,
the Gulf of Mexico and
the North Sea.

There are large amounts of oil and gas under the North Sea. The first gas field was discovered in 1959. Then oil was discovered in 1969.

The North Sea is a difficult place to drill for oil. Offshore oil rigs stand in water as deep as 180 metres. Waves can be 30 metres high and winds blow at 120 kilometres an hour.

The gas and oil is brought to the shore on oil tankers and along pipelines over 1,000 kilometres long.

Oil is brought to the surface through pipelines. It is held in storage tanks until oil tankers take it away from a filling tower. ▼

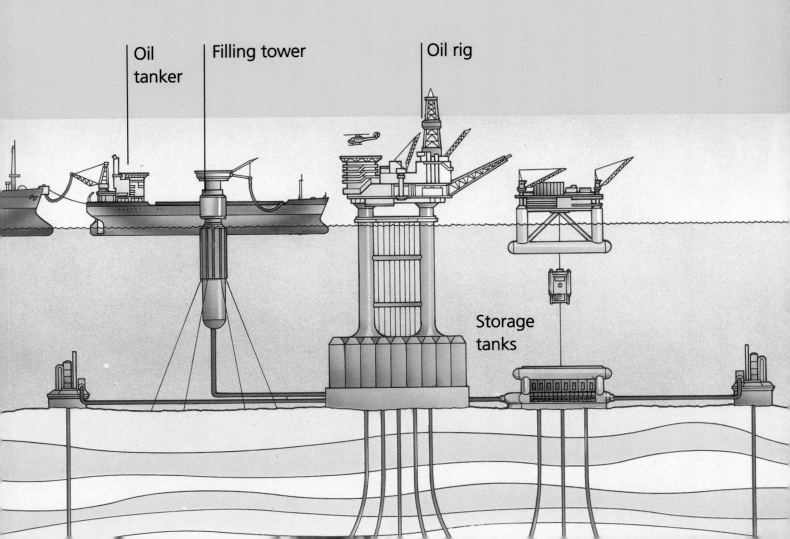

Oil tanker

Filling tower

Oil rig

Storage tanks

New oil fields

Oil companies are now prospecting, or looking for new oil fields, to the west of Scotland, where the conditions are harder.

The waves there are even bigger, and the seas are deeper. The oil rigs will have to float on the surface because the seas are so deep.

The Ekofisk oil field in the North Sea was found at the end of 1969. ▼

FACTFILE

Different oil fields produce different grades, or qualities, of oil. There are up to 100 different grades of oil around the world.

▲ An oil refinery in Puerto Rico.

Refining oil

After oil is drilled from underground, it goes to an oil refinery. Oil that comes out of the ground is called crude oil. It is only useful if it is separated into different parts. This is done in an oil refinery.

Crude oil is separated into gases, petrol, kerosene, diesel, engine oil, fuel oil, waxes and tar.

Pipelines in an oil refinery. ▼

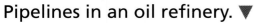

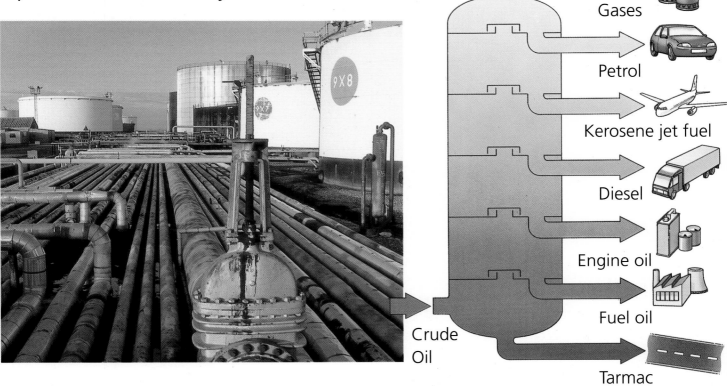

Gases

Petrol

Kerosene jet fuel

Diesel

Engine oil

Fuel oil

Crude Oil

Tarmac

Distillation

Heat, pressure and chemicals are used to distil crude oil. This separates it into different parts. At first, the oil is heated in a distillation tower.

Heat makes the lightest oils and gases rise to the top. The heavier oils stay at the bottom.

The crude oil is separated into chemicals. These can be made into plastics, detergents, fibres, medicines and other materials.

▲ A distillation tower separates crude oil into different materials. You can see the everyday products each material is used for.

An oil refinery

When oil first arrives at a refinery, it is pumped into tanks. Then it is piped into distillation towers, where it is distilled.

Next, the separated materials are piped to other parts of the refinery. They are treated to separate them even more. For example, heavy oils are cooled to remove the waxes in them. And a process called 'cracking' helps to get more petrol from heavy oil.

Finally, all the different products are put in storage tanks, ready to be sold and taken to where they will be used.

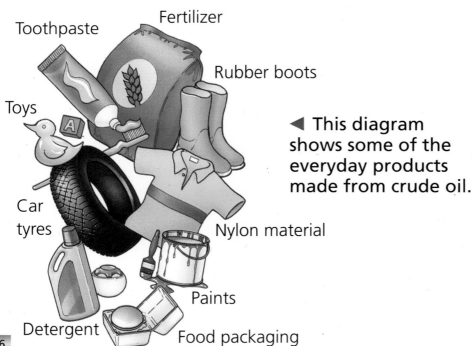

Toothpaste
Fertilizer
Rubber boots
Toys
Car tyres
Detergent
Paints
Food packaging
Nylon material

◀ This diagram shows some of the everyday products made from crude oil.

FACTFILE

The biggest oil refinery in the world is in Texas, in the USA. It can store more than 400,000 barrels of oil.

The Frederica oil refinery in Denmark. Like all refineries, this one works 24 hours a day.

▲ A tanker lorry carries products away from an oil refinery.

Moving oil

Oil is carried around the world in supertankers. Each of these huge ships can carry 400,000 tonnes of oil. On land, oil is carried in enormous pipelines. In cold countries the pipes have to be kept warm, to stop the oil getting too thick.

Moving gas

Gas from gas fields close to land is carried ashore by pipeline. But over longer distances, gas is carried by supertankers. To make it take up less space, gas is made into a liquid by cooling it to under 161.5 degrees Celsius.

Moving products

Products from oil refineries are carried by road using tanker lorries, or by rail using tanker wagons.

Supertankers are too big to enter many oil terminals. So they unload oil into smaller tankers. ▶

Supertankers carry crude oil in separate compartments, to stop the weight of the oil rolling the ship over. ▼

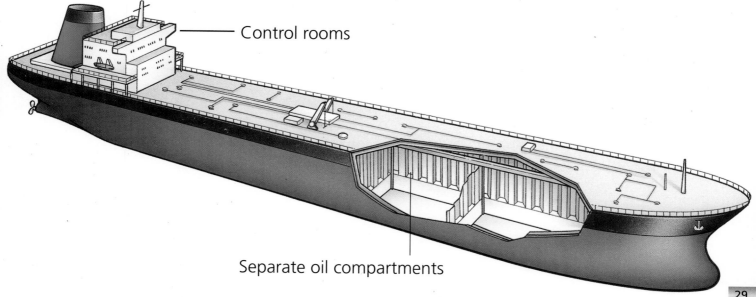

Control rooms

Separate oil compartments

Power stations in the former East Germany burned a poor grade of coal, called brown coal, or lignite. It caused serious air pollution over Europe.

Fossil fuels and the environment

When fossil fuels are burned, they release gases into the air. The gases cause air pollution and acid rain. Some scientists believe they also heat up the Earth's atmosphere, making the climate warmer.

Smog is a mixture of smoke and fog which pollutes the air. In many cities today it happens when chemicals from petrol engines mix with air. This is called photochemical smog. The weather can trap the smog over a city, making it difficult for people to breathe.

Acid rain is caused when gases from burning fossil fuels mix with water in clouds. When it rains, the water from the clouds has acid in it. The acid kills plants, damages buildings and pollutes rivers.

◀ A blue smog hangs over Hong Kong Island.

FACTFILE

In the past, most smog was caused by burning coal for heat. Today, photochemical smog is caused by car fumes.

31

On 15 February 1996, an oil-tanker called the *Sea Empress* ran aground near the coast of Wales. About 6,000 tonnes of oil spilled into the sea.

Tug boats tried to hold the tanker in place using cables. But strong gales snapped the cables and the tanker ran aground again.

Finally, six days later, the tanker was secured. By that time, over 73,000 tonnes of oil had spilled into the sea.

Cleaning up the oil spill was a huge task. In the sea, oil floats on water. So floating barriers, called booms, helped stop the oil spreading. It was skimmed off the surface and collected in tanks.

On land, it was a more difficult task. The oil was scraped off beaches and blasted off rocks using jets of water.

FACTFILE

The world's worst spill from an oil tanker was in 1979.

Two supertankers collided in the Caribbean Sea and spilled 280,000 tonnes of oil.

Workers struggle to clear crude oil from Welsh beaches, after the oil tanker *Sea Empress* ran aground in February 1996. ▶

Tug boats try to hold the *Sea Empress* in place after the tanker ran aground in February 1996. ▼

Oil and wildlife

Oil spills kill thousands of sea-birds, seals and fish. Sometimes the method of cleaning up the oil can kill as many as the actual spill. Most wildlife is poisoned by oil, and by the chemicals used to clean up the spill.

USING FOSSIL FUELS

Fossil fuels are used for energy. When they are burned, they release their energy in the form of heat.

In engines, heat from fossil fuels makes gases expand quickly. The force of this is used to make the engine work.

In the petrol engine of a car, a spark lights up petrol inside a cylinder. The heat expands the gases in the air. The force pushes a piston, which helps drive the wheels of the car.

◄ A modern petrol engine. A computer in the engine makes sure no fuel is wasted.

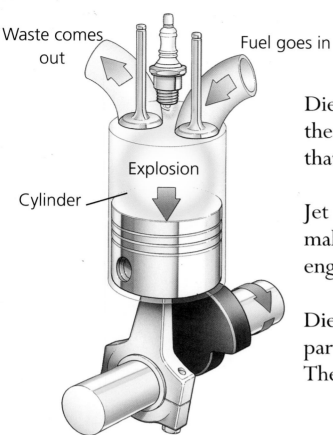

Waste comes out

Fuel goes in

Explosion

Cylinder

Diesel engines do not use a spark to light the fuel. They squeeze the fuel so much that it heats up and burns.

Jet engines burn fossil fuels. But instead of making a series of explosions like a petrol engine, they burn fuels continuously.

Diesel-electric engines are divided into two parts. A diesel engine makes electricity. The electricity makes the power.

▲ When fuel enters the petrol engine of a car, it is lit by a spark, which makes a small explosion. The explosion drives the car wheels.

This aeroplane has four jet engines, leaving trails of black smoke behind. ▼

Hot-air balloons burn propane gas to make the air inside them lighter than the air around. This helps them rise up in the air. ▶

Every day

We use fossil fuels every day. Gas is used for cooking and heating in our homes, schools and offices. Petrol and diesel help us get around. Most of our electricity is made in power stations that burn oil or coal.

Gas is very useful because it can be compressed into a small space. This makes it easy to carry around. Campers and mountaineers carry bottled gas with them to help them cook anywhere. Hot-air balloons use bottled gas to heat up the air and help them rise.

FACTFILE

Bunsen burners are gas burners. Their flame can be made bigger by letting more air mix with the gas.

▲ Some modern barbecues use piped gas, such as butane.

▲ Steam rises out of the cooling towers of Ferrybridge power station, in Yorkshire, in Britain. This is an oil-fired power station.

Power stations

Not all power stations burn fossil fuels. Some use nuclear, wind or water power. But most power stations burn coal or oil.

In coal-fired power stations, heat from burning coal turns water into steam. The steam drives the generators that make electricity.

Coal and oil-fired power stations burn hundreds of tonnes of coal and oil every day. So coal-fired power stations are usually built near coal fields, and oil-fired power stations are usually built near oil refineries.

Waste

Power stations that burn fossil fuels waste a lot of energy. More heat is made from burning fuels than is used to heat the water. Most of this heat is not used.

Some power stations in Scandinavia use the extra heat. Special pipes under the power stations carry the heat to homes and offices.

FACTFILE

Most of Britain's energy comes from fossil fuels. Oil makes about 46 per cent, coal makes about 28 per cent and gas makes 19 per cent.

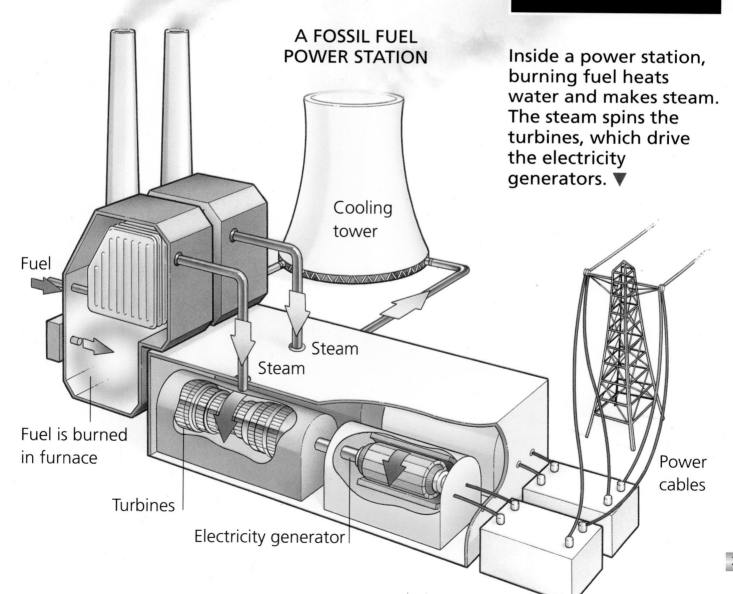

A FOSSIL FUEL POWER STATION

Inside a power station, burning fuel heats water and makes steam. The steam spins the turbines, which drive the electricity generators. ▼

Cooling tower

Fuel

Steam

Steam

Fuel is burned in furnace

Turbines

Electricity generator

Power cables

Before the 1980s, Denmark's main fuels were oil and coal. Oil was expensive because it was imported from the Middle East.

In 1959, natural gas fields were discovered in the North Sea. If the country could use gas instead of oil it would be much cheaper. So in 1979, Denmark started to build pipelines to carry gas from the North Sea.

Gas is a cleaner fuel to burn than coal or oil. By burning gas instead of oil, Denmark has lowered its levels of air pollution.

FACTFILE

Half of all Danish homes are now heated by gas piped from the North Sea.

This map shows Denmark's gas and oil pipelines. ▼

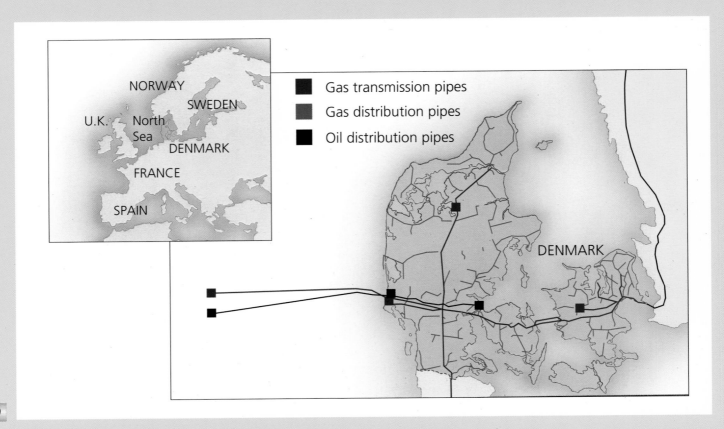

NORWAY
SWEDEN
U.K.   North Sea
DENMARK
FRANCE
SPAIN

■ Gas transmission pipes
■ Gas distribution pipes
■ Oil distribution pipes

DENMARK

Coal

Coal is still one of Denmark's main fuels. Most of it is burned in power stations to make electricity.

When it is burned, coal makes more carbon dioxide than any other fossil fuel. This causes air pollution and may help to warm the Earth's climate. So Denmark is trying to use wind power instead of coal, to make electricity.

◄ Gas pipelines being laid in Denmark. The pipelines have to run under many small seas in this country.

◄ This power station burns coal to make electricity. It also makes heat, which is carried away in hot water and used to heat people's homes.

THE FUTURE

Burning fossil fuels pollutes the Earth's environment. Fossil fuels are also running out.
We need to find cleaner ways of burning fossil fuels.
We also need to find different kinds of power to use in their place.

Cutting down pollution

Power stations can lower pollution from coal by using special equipment in their chimneys. This equipment takes out harmful substances from the waste gases as they pass through the chimney.

Pollution from cars can be reduced by using catalytic converters. These lower the amount of harmful gases produced by the engine. Cars can also use unleaded petrol instead of leaded petrol. Petrol with lead in it makes poisonous gases when it is burned.

Using less fuel also cuts down pollution. Public transport such as buses and trains uses less fuel per person than cars. So if we use more public transport, we can help to cut down air pollution. Governments can help by making public transport better and cheaper.

▲ Coal that is made into a liquid has less sulphur than solid coal. This means it is a cleaner fuel to burn. It causes less air pollution.

There is much more coal left in the world than oil or gas. So once oil and gas run out, coal may be used even more. We must find cleaner ways of using it.

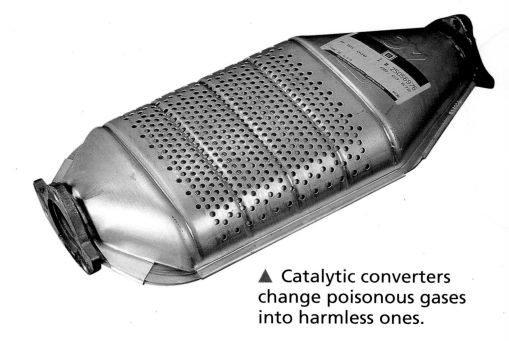

▲ Catalytic converters change poisonous gases into harmless ones.

Petrol pumps coloured green have unleaded petrol. In many countries, unleaded petrol is the only petrol allowed. ▼

This car uses hydrogen instead of petrol. ▶

New fuels

Hydrogen is a gas that can be used as a fuel. When it burns, it makes water vapour instead of harmful gases. So it is much cleaner than coal or oil.

Hydrogen can be made from fossil fuels. But it can also be made from water. This means that when fossil fuels run out, it will still be possible to make hydrogen fuel.

Scientists are trying to find ways of using more hydrogen instead of fossil fuels. One way is to use it in fuel cells.

A diagram of
a fuel cell. ▼

▲ This engineer is putting fuel
cells together.

Electricity

Hydrogen (H_2)

Oxygen (O_2)

Water
(H_2O)

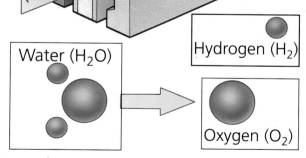

Water (H_2O)

Hydrogen (H_2)

Oxygen (O_2)

Hydrogen (H_2)

▲ Water can be
split into hydrogen
and oxygen. The
chemical symbol for each
substance is in brackets.

Fuel cells and electric cars

A fuel cell mixes hydrogen and oxygen to
make electricity. The only waste product
is water. So fuel cells are a very clean
source of power.

Fuel cells are very expensive. But
if they could be made cheaper, they could
be used in electric cars in the future.

GLOSSARY

Acid rain Rain that contains pollution from factories and traffic.

Atmosphere The gases that surround the Earth.

Booms Floating barriers, used to stop oil-spills spreading in the sea.

Butane A colourless gas made from crude oil in a refinery.

Compressed Squashed.

Crude oil Pure oil that has just come from underground.

Cylinder An object shaped like a roller or tube, which can be hollow or solid.

Density Thickness or compactness.

Distil Purify by heating up and then cooling down.

Environment Everything in our surroundings: the earth, air and water.

Expand To grow larger.

Extracted Taken out.

Generators Machines that make electricity.

Grades Different qualities of something.

Gravity The natural force that attracts objects towards the centre of the Earth.

Imported Brought in from a foreign country.

Magnetic field The area around a magnet where its power of attraction works.

Microscopic Objects that cannot be seen without using a microscope.

Mummies Dead bodies that have been specially treated to stop them decaying.

Piston Two cylinders, one inside the other, that go up and down. Pistons are used to make engines or pumps work.

Pollute To make dirty.

Propane gas A colourless gas made from oil or natural gas.

Prospecting Exploring an area to look for oil, gold or other minerals.

Refinery A building used to distill crude oil. There are also sugar and metal refineries, used to purify sugar and metal.

Sedimentary rocks Rocks formed from material that has been deposited by water, wind or ice.

Surveying Examining an area.

Tar sand Sand covered with a substance that produces oil.

Terminal Either end of a route where goods are loaded or unloaded.

Turbines Engines or motors that are made to work by the power of water, steam or air.

Waste The substances left over after something has been used.

FURTHER INFORMATION

Books to read

Alpha Science: Energy by Sally Morgan (Evans, 1997)

A Closer Look at the Greenhouse Effect by Alex Edmonds (Watts, 1999)

Cycles in Science: Energy by Peter D.Riley (Heinemann, 1997)

Earth Watch: Acid Rain, Changing Climate & Ozone Hole by Sally Morgan (Watts, 1999)

Energy Forever series: Fossil Fuels, Geothermal and Bio-Energy, Nuclear Power, Solar Power, Water Power, Wind Power (Hodder Wayland, 1998)

Future Tech: Energy by Sally Morgan (Belitha, 1999)

Living for the Future: Energy and Resources by Paul Brown (Watts, 1998)

Protecting our Planet: Fuels for the Future by Steve Parker (Hodder Wayland, 1997)

Saving Our World: New Energy Sources by N.Hawkes (Watts, 2000)

Science Topics: Energy by Chris Oxlade (Heinemann, 1998)

Step-by-Step Science: Energy and Movement by Chris Oxlade (Watts, 1998)

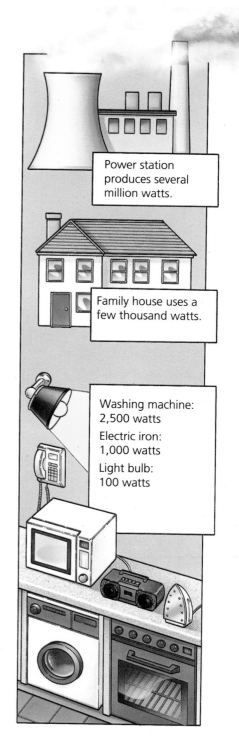

Power station produces several million watts.

Family house uses a few thousand watts.

Washing machine: 2,500 watts

Electric iron: 1,000 watts

Light bulb: 100 watts

ENERGY CONSUMPTION

The use of energy is measured in joules per second, or watts. Different machines use up different amounts of energy. The diagram on the right gives a few examples. ▶

INDEX